# FAVOURITE
# CARAVAN AND
# MOTORHOME
## RECIPES

*compiled by*
## Cindy Thompson

*Illustrated with*
*nostalgic photographs*

**SALMON**

# Index

*With thanks to Andrew Jenkinson – caravan/motorhome journalist and historian
for sourcing the images used in this publication.*

Printed and published by J. Salmon Ltd., Sevenoaks, England © Copyright

# Beef with Creamy Mustard Sauce

**1 lb. braising steak     10 cherry tomatoes**
**1 tablespoon Dijon mustard     Tub of cream**
**2 tablespoons olive oil     3 tablespoons water**
**Salt and freshly ground multi-coloured pepper**

Heat oil in deep pan which has a lid. Season the steak well with salt and a good coating of pepper. Fry steak until sealed. Add tomatoes (or onions or mushrooms) and turn down heat to low and cover with lid for 30–40 minutes until tender. When steak is tender, serve on plate, turn up heat, then add a little water to pan if needed. Then add mustard, then cream, mix well and serve on top of steak. Serves 2.

NB.  A small thinly sliced onion or a tin of mushrooms can replace the tomatoes.

# Chicken or Turkey Schnitzel

**4 boneless fillets of chicken (or turkey)**
**2 cloves of garlic   1 egg, beaten**
**2 oz. matzo meal (could use flour or breadcrumbs instead)**
**Paprika   Salt and black pepper   Juice of lemon**
**Flour for dusting   1 tablespoon water   Oil for frying**

Place the fillets between two pieces of greaseproof paper and pound with a mallet or rolling pin to about half its original thickness. Marinade the meat in lemon juice, garlic, salt and pepper in a bowl. Arrange 3 bowls in a row and put in the first some flour, in the second the beaten egg and water, and in the third the matzo meal or breadcrumbs, with salt, pepper and paprika. Quickly dip each fillet in turn in all three bowls, then put the coated meat on a plate and chill for at least 30 minutes. In a large heavy frying pan heat the oil until a cube of bread will turn golden brown when dropped into it. Fry the fillets until golden brown on each side. Drain on kitchen paper and serve with vegetables.

Large fillets could serve 4, small fillets serve 2.

# Lentil Soup

**3 tablespoons olive oil   2 celery sticks, chopped**
**6 garlic cloves, chopped   1 cup of red lentils**
**2 bay leaves   ⅓ teaspoon ground cumin**
**1 onion, finely chopped   1-2 carrots, chopped**
**1 potato, peeled and chopped   1 litre of vegetable stock**
**1-2 lemons, halved   Salt and pepper**
**Cayenne pepper or Tabasco sauce to taste**
**Coriander or parsley leaves to garnish**

Heat oil in a large deep pan and fry onion until soft. Add celery, carrots, half the garlic, and all the potato, cook until beginning to soften. Add lentils and stock to pan and bring to the boil. Then reduce the heat and simmer for about 30 minutes until potato and lentils are tender, adding more water if necessary. Add the bay leaves, salt and pepper to taste, remaining garlic and half the lemons to the pan. Cook for a further 10 minutes. Remove the bay leaves and squeeze the juice from the remaining lemons to taste. Pour soup into blender or just mix well. Stir in the cumin pepper or Tabasco. Serve garnished with parsley or coriander. Serves 3 to 4.

# Liver and Onions

**Pack of liver**   **⅓ cup of flour**
**2 large onions**   **Salt and pepper to taste**
**¼ cup paprika**   **1 tablespoon soy sauce**
**2 teaspoons gravy granules**   **Oil for frying**
**A little water**

Put flour and paprika into a bowl or a bag. Add salt and pepper to season. Cut liver up into manageable pieces, then put each one into the flour and coat well. Heat some oil up in a thick frying pan and fry the liver until just cooked. Take each piece out when done and put to one side in a dish. Fry the onions with the last batch of liver, then when cooked, add some water to the pan, soy sauce and all the fried liver. The water at this point should thicken up due to the flour used on the liver. Add the gravy granules to thicken the gravy further and cook on low heat for a further 10 minutes. Serve with mashed potato and greens. Serves 2.

# One Pot Stew with Sage Dumplings

**1 lb. cubed meat (either stewing steak, pork or lamb)**
**2 onions, roughly cut   2 large carrots, roughly cut**
**1 stick celery, diced   2 tablespoons of peas**
**2 cloves garlic   1 tablespoon of soy sauce**
**2 oxo cubes   1 heaped tablespoon paprika**
**1 tablespoon oil   Rind and juice of lemon**
**3 tablespoons seasoned flour   Salt and pepper**

**Dumplings**
**15-20 fresh sage leaves   4 oz. self-raising flour   2 oz. suet**
**Approximately 5 tablespoons cold water   Pinch of salt**

Coat cubed meat well in seasoned flour. Heat oil in a large heavy pan and fry meat until sealed. Add roughly cut onions and carrots and garlic and fry for a couple of minutes. Turn heat down and add soy sauce, diced celery, oxo cubes, paprika, rind and juice of lemon, and enough water to almost cover the ingredients. Cover and cook for 40 minutes. Mix flour, suet, salt and sage water to a firm but pliable dough. Divide into 4 large dumplings. Add peas and dumplings and check there is enough water. Cover and cook for a further 20 minutes. Blitz sage leaves with water in a hand processor (or chop very finely with a knife). Serves 2.

*Eight*

# Pasta and Tuna Bake

**Tin of tuna chunks in oil    1 red/green pepper**
**1 tablespoon oil from tuna    2 teaspoons paprika**
**Cup of double cream    6 oz. grated cheese**
**1 onion    1 teaspoon chilli    Salt and pepper**
**10 cherry tomatoes    2 cups of pasta or macaroni**

Cook macaroni or pasta, drain and set aside.  In a thick pan fry onion in oil until transparent, then add sliced pepper.  Season with salt and pepper then add paprika, chilli and tomatoes.  Finely add tin of tuna.  Add cream and when hot add grated cheese.  Mix pasta into cream mix and serve, or put in hot oven with extra grated cheese on top.  Serves 2.

# Pepper Steak

**2 fillet or sirloin steaks (braising steak can also be used)**
**Black peppercorns to coat steaks, crushed**
**1 tablespoon butter    2 tablespoons vegetable oil**
**¼ pint whipping cream    Salt to taste**
**(Optional: 1 garlic clove or cherry tomatoes or mushrooms or onions)**

Coat steaks in crushed peppercorns and sprinkle with a little salt. Heat oil in thick saucepan and seal fry the meat both sides to your tastes. If using braising steak, seal fry the meat then turn heat right down and put pan over a diffuser and cook for at least an hour until tender. When the meat is nearly cooked you can add the optional crushed garlic or tomatoes or mushrooms. Take meat out of pan and add cream and butter to juices. Put meat back in pan to coat the meat, then serve with potatoes and vegetables. Serves 2.

# Quick Chicken Korma

**4 chicken fillets    1 large onion, chopped**
**1 large carrot, chopped    Juice of half a lemon/lime**
**2 tablespoons peas    Cup of cream or yoghurt**
**2 tablespoons of chosen curry paste**
**Water as needed    Oil for frying**
**Fresh coriander**

Cut chicken into large pieces and fry gently until sealed, then add chopped onion, peas and carrot. Fry until just cooked. Add curry paste to pan and juice of lemon or lime. Simmer, adding water if needed until flavours are infused and well mixed. A few minutes before serving, add yoghurt or cream and warm through, making sure the ingredients are mixed well. Adding the cream or yoghurt will greatly tone down the strong flavours of the curry and is a good step to rectify a curry that is too strong. Garnish with freshly chopped coriander and serve with rice and flat bread. Serves 2, but adding extra bread and a little salad will easily serve 4.

# Soufflé Pancakes

**4 oz. flour    16 fl. oz. milk**
**2 oz. butter, melted**
**6 egg whites, beaten stiff**
**6 egg yolks    Butter for frying**
**Sugar    Salt**

Prepare batter from flour, salt, milk and egg yolks.  Add melted butter and beat.  Gradually fold egg whites into batter.  Melt butter in a pan.  Pour in 1 cm thickness of batter.  Fry until golden on both sides.  Tear pancake into 1 inch square pieces and fry all over.  Serve hot sprinkled with sugar.  Can add sultanas if liked.  Serves 2.

# Babouts

*A recipe from Morocco, where it is used to accompany cheese, butter and honey.*

**8 oz. wheat flour**
**4 oz. white flour**
**¼ teaspoon salt**
**1 soup spoon of yeast**
**1 large glass of tepid water**

Activate yeast as necessary. Mix the flours, salt and yeast in a large bowl, then gradually add the tepid water to make a dough. Knead dough for about 5 minutes, then roll out to about 1½ inch thickness, and cut out circles of about 2 inches. Arrange on trays and lightly sprinkle with flour and leave to rise. Fry in lightly greased thick pan until both sides are brown and the babouts have puffed up.

# Butterscotch Biscuits

**4 oz. butter**
**½ cup brown sugar**
**2 cups of self-raising flour**
**1 teaspoon vanilla essence**
**1 tablespoon golden syrup**

Beat butter, essence, sugar and golden syrup in a bowl with an electric whisk until light and fluffy. Stir in the sifted flour to make a workable dough. Roll small teaspoon-sized balls of mixture and place on a greased baking tray about 2 inches apart. Bake at 300°F or Mark 2 for about 20 minutes or until firm to touch. Makes about 75 biscuits.

# Basic Bread

**1 lb. 2 oz. strong white bread flour**
**¾ pint tepid water**
**1⅓ teaspoon salt**
**⅓ oz. fresh yeast (or 1 x 7g packet of easy-blend yeast, activate as necessary)**

Mix flour and salt in a large bowl (if possible warm the flour up a little as this will help the yeast to work faster).  If using fresh yeast, crumble into some tepid water (1 part boiling to 2 parts cold.  The resulting water should be warm to the hand) mix and leave to stand for a few minutes.  Once the yeast has mixed evenly, pour over flour and add the remaining water slowly as you mix with your hands.  Work the dough until it leaves the sides of the bowl and your hands are left clean. If the dough is a little sticky, add an additional tablespoon of flour, if the dough is dry, add a tablespoon of water and work some more.  Turn the dough out onto a lightly floured surface or onto a large round tray to keep the mess to a minimum.  The dough has to be stretched to develop its elasticity and to allow a good rise.  To knead, use the heel of your hand and push the dough away from you, stretching it as you do.  Then fold it back on itself and start again.  To test if the dough is kneaded enough, take a small piece between your thumb and forefinger and squash it.  The dough should be very elastic and squashed to an almost translucent paper thinness. Return the dough to the bowl and cover with clingfilm, or lid, or a tea towel and leave to rise until double its size. This will take 1 hour in a warm place, 1½ hours in a cooler place, or overnight in the fridge. When the dough has risen properly, it will not spring back when you poke it with your finger. Put the dough onto a lightly floured surface or your tray and punch it down and knead lightly again. This redistributes the air bubbles and makes an evenly fluffed loaf of bread. Shape into one large loaf and put dough into a greased 2 lb. loaf tin or cut in half and place into two greased 1 lb. loaf tins. Leave somewhere warm and cover with a plastic bag and tie closed, allowing room for the dough to rise again. You must allow 40 minutes to 1 hour for this stage. Preheat oven to 425°F or Mark 7. When the dough has risen, take out of the bag and make a couple of cuts across the top of each loaf. Bake for about 35 minutes. The bread will be baked when you can make a hollow sound from tapping the loaf on the underside. Allow to cool before cutting.

# Caribbean Fried Dumplings

*I discovered these dumplings whilst living in Barbados. For a camper they make a really good emergency bread, which I have used often camped in the middle of nowhere!*

**1 lb. self-raising flour**
**½ teaspoon salt**
**1 teaspoon sugar**
**½ pint milk**
**Oil for frying**

Sift the dry ingredients together in a large bowl and add the milk to make a workable dough. Knead until smooth, then divide into 10 balls. Press each ball into rounds no more than just over ⅜ inch thick. Any thicker than this and they do not cook easily in the middle. Fry dumplings in heavy frying pan both sides until brown puffed up and cooked through. Serve as you would scones or use as bread.

# Irish Soda Bread

**1½ lbs. flour (can use 1 lb. wholemeal/½ lb. plain white)**
**¼ tablespoon bicarbonate of soda**
**8 fl. oz. buttermilk or sour milk**
**¼ teaspoon salt**

Preheat oven to 400°F or Mark 6. Mix all dry ingredients. Make a well in the centre. Stir in milk vigorously to make a rough dough. On floured board, flatten dough to 1½ inch thickness. Make a cross on the dough, brush with milk and bake for 40 minutes.

# M'smmens

*A North African dish, they can be left plain or mincemeat can be placed inside the folded dough. Either way, they are easy to make and delicious.*

**2 large cereal-sized bowls of wheat flour**
**1 large cereal bowl of white flour**
**1 teaspoon salt   ½ glass oil**
**½ glass soft butter   16 fl. oz. tepid water**

Mix the flours, salt and water well into a non-sticky workable dough. Divide dough into large egg-sized balls. Dip your fingers in the oil and take each piece of dough in turn and pat out into a circle of about 8 inch diameter. Take a little of the soft butter and smear over the circle, then fold the opposite sides of the circle into the middle. (At this point you could add a small amount of mincemeat spiced with salt, pepper, finely chopped onion, chopped coriander, cumin, and paprika. This makes an extra special accompaniment to a rice or a soup dish.) Smear the middle of the dough with butter and fold the top of the dough over, then smear butter on the remaining free area and fold the bottom of the dough up to form a square. Pat down again to about a 4 inch square. Sprinkle the dough squares with a little of the wheat flour. Fry the squares in a well-oiled thick pan until cooked brown on both sides. Whilst one is cooking you can be flattening out the next one. Makes roughly 8 to 10.

# Chick's Spicy Meatballs

**1 lb. mincemeat    2 eggs    1 medium onion, finely chopped**
**3 oz. breadcrumbs    1 clove crushed garlic (optional)**
**1 desert spoon paprika    2 teaspoons crushed fresh chilli**
**2 teaspoons lemon juice**
**1 desert spoon of either steak seasoning or BBQ seasoning**
**Salt and pepper to taste    1 tablespoon sunflower oil**

Put mincemeat into a large bowl and add garlic, onion, spices, lemon juice and eggs. Mix lightly with a spoon, then start adding slowly the breadcrumbs. You will need to mix with your fingers to get a good firm mix that holds together when formed into a ball. Roll mixture into small egg-sized meatballs and put on a plate. You might find that keeping your hands wet with cold water will help this. Fry the meatballs and turn to cook on a medium heat, taking out the ones that are cooked. For quickness I use any well-known brand of tomato pasta sauce base for the sauce. Put all the meatballs back into the pan and add the sauce. Season to taste. Serve with rice or flat bread. Easily serves 4.

# Moist Carrot Cake

**6 oz. dark brown sugar     ½ lb. wholemeal self-raising flour**
**1 tablespoon treacle     2 large eggs**
**1½ teaspoons bicarbonate of soda**
**4 fl. oz. sunflower oil     ½ lb. grated carrots**
**3 teaspoons mixed spice     Zest of 1 orange**
**6 oz sultanas (or mixed fruit)**

**Syrup Glaze**
**Juice of half a small orange**
**2 oz. dark brown sugar**
**1 teaspoon lemon juice**

Preheat oven to 325°F or Mark 3.  Mix eggs, sugar and oil together.  Sift flour, bicarbonate of soda and spice into a bowl.  Stir egg mixture with flour, then fold in zest, carrots and sultanas.  Put mixture into a greased tin 10 inch x 6 inch and bake for 35–40 minutes.  For the glaze, mix everything together and when the cake comes out of the oven, stab with fork and slowly pour juice over the cake.

# Moroccan Yogurt Pot Cake

*This very easy cake doesn't need scales or an oven, just a yogurt pot!*
*All measurements are taken as 1 full yogurt pot (except eggs)*

**2 small tubs yogurt   2 tubs sugar   2 tubs sunflower oil   2 eggs**
**4 tubs flour (plain flour + 2 teaspoons of baking powder)   2 teaspoons of vanilla sugar**

**Optional**
**1 tub cocoa powder or grated rind of lemon/orange + juice**
**1 tub sultanas/raisins/chocolate drops**
***In fact you could add 1 tub of any type of flavouring (banana, pear, etc.)***

Whisk yogurt in a bowl and then whisk in the sugar and then the sunflower oil. Whisk in the eggs one at a time. Then whisk in first measure of flour with vanilla sugar/baking powder, with optional flavourings.

Grease a Moroccan cake tin adding greaseproof paper on bottom of tin. Add mixture to tin and cook over a diffuser on lowest hot setting for at least 45 minutes (sometimes takes longer). Can also be baked in a skillet over a diffuser.

Or put into greased 8 inch cake tin and bake in moderate oven 350°F or mark 4 for about 35–45 minutes.

# Peanut Butter Biscuits

*These are really quick-to-make biscuits, but they never last very long once cooked!*

**9 oz. crunchy peanut butter**
**5 oz. golden caster sugar**
**2-3 drops of vanilla essence (or 1 sachet of vanilla sugar)**
**1 large egg, beaten**

Put peanut butter and sugar in a bowl and mix well. Add the vanilla essence and egg and mix well, until the mixture is very stiff. Divide the dough into roughly 24 pieces and roll them into balls and space them apart on greased baking trays. With a wet fork, squash the biscuits down a little to make a ridged pattern. Bake in a preheated oven 350°F or Mark 4 for 12–15 minutes until golden brown.

# Quick Cream Cake

*This cake was given to me by a German friend.*
*It has a Madeira sponge texture, a little dry, but you can add less flour if you like.*

**½ lb. margarine    6 oz. sugar    14 oz. flour**
**1 teaspoon or sachet of baking powder**
**2 teaspoon or sachet vanilla sugar**
**3 eggs**
**Cream or milk to make softer mix**

Cream sugar and margarine until soft and fluffy. Add eggs one at a time. Mix vanilla sugar, flour and baking powder, then fold into creamed mix. Add enough cream or milk to make a smoother cake mixture. Put into 8 inch tin or into two sponge tins and bake at 350°F or Mark 4 for 30–45 minutes or until a skewer comes out clean.

Of course you can add flavourings of sultanas or cocoa powder. You can also sandwich the cakes with jam and whipped cream. This makes a very good result for a quick birthday cake on the road.

# Sesame Biscuits

*These biscuits are popular in Morocco and are very easy and tasty.*

**1 lb. sesame seeds (blitz them in a small grinder)**
**2 eggs    1 tablespoon flour**
**9 oz. icing sugar (caster sugar will suffice)**
**1 teaspoon or sachet baking powder**
**1 tablespoon jam    4 tablespoons melted butter**

***For decoration* – Orange flower water and icing sugar**

Wash and dry the sesame seeds, then brown them in a lightly oiled pan. You can instead buy toasted sesame seeds. In a mixer blend everything except the butter, or mix with a spoon. Add butter to make a dough that is workable. Make walnut-sized balls and then roll in orange water, then in the icing sugar, then place on a greased baking tray. Bake at 350°F or Mark 4 for 15 minutes until the biscuits have formed a slight crust.

If you do not want to use 1 lb. sesame seeds, you could make these biscuits with ½ lb. sesame and ½ lb. flour.

Makes about 25 to 30 biscuits.

# Traveller's Christmas Cake

*I always make my Christmas cake sometime before the end of September and then spend the months before Christmas feeding the cake with brandy.*

**½ lb. butter, softened    4 eggs    ½ lb. soft brown sugar    3 tablespoons marmalade**
**1.5 kg mixed dried fruit *(this can include chopped dates, apricots, etc.)***
**2½ oz. self-raising flour    ½ lb. plain flour**
**4 teaspoons mixed spice    ½ cup brandy or rum or sherry**

Heat in a saucepan the dried fruit and brandy so that the fruit can absorb the brandy. Leave to cool. Preheat oven to 300°F or Mark 2 and line and grease a deep 7½ inch square cake tin or two loaf tins. Beat butter and sugar in a large bowl until just combined. Beat in eggs roughly one at a time. Don't worry if it curdles. Add marmalade and fruit and mix well with your hand. Sift spice and flours over mixture. Mix well. If too wet add a little more flour, if dry add a little more brandy or sherry, or even rum if you prefer! Spoon into baking tin, making sure that the corners are filled with the cake mixture. Bake for about 3 hours until skewer comes out clean. Once the cake has cooked, prick the top with a knife or a skewer and "feed" the cake with a few spoonfuls of your chosen spirit about once every week and wrap in foil and keep in an airtight container. By the time Christmas arrives, we always have a fabulously rich and moist cake. I never cover it with icing, but of course you could.

# Lebanese Flat Bread

*This recipe can be baked in a skillet if you don't have an oven.*

**6 cups of plain flour   1½ teaspoon salt   2 tablespoons oil   1 teaspoon sugar**
**1 sachet of active dried yeast or ½ inch cube of fresh yeast   2 cups of warm water**

Sift warm flour into bowl and remove about 2 cups of flour. Activate dried yeast, or dissolve fresh yeast in ¼ cup of warm water, add remaining water, sugar and salt. Mix well. Pour yeast mixture over flour. Mix to make a thick liquid. Cover and leave in warm place until frothy (about ½ hour). Stir in remaining flour and oil. Knead for 10 minutes. The dough is ready when it has a smooth, satiny and slightly wrinkled texture. Lightly oil bowl and bread and place back in the bowl, cover with cling film or plastic bag and leave in a warm place until doubled in size (about 1½ hours). Punch down the dough and knead for 2 minutes. Divide into 8 equal pieces and roll each into roughly 8 inch rounds or small enough to fit skillet. Place on a lightly floured surface. Alternately, push the dough flat. Cover with oiled plastic and roll out the next. And so on. Heat skillet using other pan as a cover. Just before baking, turn heat down to medium, wipe quickly the base with very light coating of oil and add the round of bread, closing skillet quickly. Bake for 3 minutes until puffed but not burnt on under side, then turn round over, recover and cook for further 2 minutes or until bread has cooked through. If baking in oven preheat to 450°F or Mark 8 for 15 minutes. Makes 8 breads.

# One Mix Sponge Cake

*You can't get an easier cake than this to make. All the ingredients are simply thrown into a large bowl and whisked with a hand whisk! You can make any flavour of cake you like, cocoa, marmalade, etc. Just add a tablespoonful of flavouring in with the mixture.*

**6 oz. soft margarine/butter**
**6 oz. self-raising flour**
**6 oz. caster sugar**
**1 teaspoon baking power**
**3 eggs**

Preheat oven to 350°F or Mark 4 and grease two 7 inch sandwich tins, lining the bases. Place all the ingredients into a large bowl and with a hand whisk beat for 2 to 3 minutes until smooth. Divide mixture between tins. Bake for about 25 minutes or until well risen and a skewer comes out clean. Cool tins for 5 minutes then turn out on wire rack. When cool, sandwich together with whipped cream, lemon curd or jam.

# Yogurt Lemon Cake

*This moist sponge takes a lot of beating and whisking, but worth the effort.*

**3 eggs**
**11 oz. caster sugar**
**2 oz. butter**
**8 oz. natural thick set yogurt**
**1 teaspoon vanilla essence**
**Zest of lemon**
**6 oz. self-raising flour**

Preheat oven to 350°F or Mark 4 and grease and line an 8 inch round cake tin. In a large bowl put yolks, butter, sugar and beat until pale and fluffy. Add yogurt, lemon zest, vanilla essence and beat again until smooth. Fold in sifted flour. In a separate bowl whisk egg whites until soft peaks form. Carefully fold in the egg whites into the cake mixture and pour into cake tin. Bake for about 1 hour until sponge has risen well and a skewer comes out clean. Allow to cool, then dust with icing sugar.

# Cheese Gougères

*A scrummy version of this Northern hearty delight.*

**1 pint milk   4 oz. soft margarine**
**1-2 teaspoons salt   White pepper**
**Nutmeg   8 oz. flour   7 eggs**
**2 tablespoons double cream**
**4 oz. Gougère cheese (Cheddar can be used), finely chopped**

Bring milk, margarine, salt, pepper and nutmeg to the boil. Add all the flour at once and keep stirring until the dough comes away from the sides of the pan and forms a ball. Remove from heat and stir in one egg and allow to cool a little. Stir in the remaining eggs one by one, then add the cheese and cream. Break off small pieces of dough with two tablespoons and place them on a greased baking tray, lined with parchment. Bake in preheated oven 425°F or Mark 7 for 25 to 30 minutes. Makes approximately 40 gougères.

# Egyptian Rice

*This recipe I discovered whilst travelling in Egypt and visiting a Korshari house.*
*Korshari is a very popular, cheap, layered vegetarian dish that is served with garlic and*
*chilli sauce. The layers are macaroni, rice, lentils, onions, pine nuts and thin potato chips.*
*This dish is often sold from wheeled street carts, as many people eat from street traders in*
*Egypt. I have taken the rice, macaroni, onions and nuts from this dish, to make an*
*interesting change to plain rice.*

**1 cupful of basmati rice    1 cup of macaroni**
**1 large onion, thinly sliced**
**½ cup pine nuts, roughly chopped**
**2 cups of water    Sunflower oil**

Wash the rice and drain, mix with the macaroni and put into a covered
saucepan with almost 2 cups of water. Bring to the boil and simmer for 10
minutes over a diffuser. Meanwhile, fry the very thinly sliced onion until they
start to turn brown, then add the roughly chopped pine nuts. Continue to fry
the onions until they are almost black. Add to the rice and mix roughly.
Serves 2.

# Gypsy Toast

*An idea to use up the stale bread which always seems to be accumulated by campers.*

**Slices of stale white or brown bread**
**¼ pint milk    1 oz. butter**
**4 oz. grated cheese    1 egg**
**Pepper**

Beat egg and milk in a bowl adding pepper to taste.  Put some butter in a pan.
Soak each slice of bread in the egg mixture and fry until golden on both sides.
Add grated cheese to one side whilst in the frying pan.

# Sauerkraut

*This is a recipe that is popular with our German friends on the road.  Whenever we have a get together they always make this dish for us to share.  You must make it at least the day before to allow time for the cabbage to soak up the juices.*

**1 medium hard cabbage    1 medium onion
1 cup of sherry or malt vinegar    2 cups of sunflower oil
8 tablespoons sugar    3 cups of soda water
Salt and pepper to taste**

Shred cabbage and onion into a large bowl, preferably with a lid.  One of those magic hand-held slicers and dicers is perfect for this.  Add other ingredients and mix well.  Add salt and pepper to taste.  You will need more salt and pepper than you think to create a good taste, so don't be afraid to add too much.  Keep in a fridge over night.  This dish will keep at least a week.  You can use red cabbage if you like.

# Bread and Butter Pudding

*A traditional favourite to use up stale bread.*

**1 tablespoon butter, softened    4-5 slices white/brown bread**
**Rind of 1 lemon    4 tablespoons marmalade**
**4 oz. raisins or sultanas    1½ oz. mixed peel**
**1 teaspoon cinnamon or mixed spice**
**3 oz. brown sugar    3 eggs    1 pint milk**
**2 tablespoons demerara sugar**
**1 cooking apple, grated (optional)**

Grease an ovenproof dish with butter and with the remainder spread over the slices of bread.  Place a layer of bread at the base of the dish, coat with half the marmalade, and sprinkle with half the sultanas, lemon rind, mixed peel, spice, brown sugar and all of the apple.  Add another layer of bread, coat with rest of marmalade and cover with most of the remaining sultanas, all of the remaining peel, brown sugar, and spice.  Add the final layer of bread.  Lightly beat the eggs and the milk and pour over the bread in the dish.  Leave to stand for a few minutes.  Finish off by sprinkling the top with demerara sugar and the remaining sultanas.  Bake in a preheated oven 400°F or Mark 6 for 50–60 minutes, until risen and golden brown.  Can be eaten hot or cold.

# Lemon Mousse

*Made with a hand-held whisk, this recipe is impressive.*

**3 oz. packet of lemon flavoured jelly crystals**
**2 teaspoons gelatine   ½ cup cold water**
**12 oz. can evaporated milk**
**2 egg whites, lightly beaten**

Mix the gelatine in the water in a cup and stand the cup in a pan of simmering water with jelly crystals.  Stir well until dissolved.  Combine the milk and gelatine mixture in a bowl and put in the fridge to cool for about an hour, or until just beginning to set.  Stir in the egg whites and mix with an electric hand whisk for about 5–10 minutes, or until light and fluffy and doubled in bulk. Put into family-sized trifle bowl and keep in the fridge for a couple of hours until set.

Makes 4 small desserts.

# Unbaked Fruit Slice

*This is a very quick and easy desert and can be made a couple of days before needed.*

**2 teaspoons gelatine**
**1 tablespoon water**
**8 oz. ricotta cheese**
**⅓ cup natural yogurt**
**½ cup icing sugar**
**⅓ cup chosen fruit, mashed**
**Packet of sweet biscuits or trifle fingers**

Line a 7½ inch square baking tray with foil. Place biscuits in the bottom of the tray, trimming to fit. Put gelatine in cup with water and stand in a pan of simmering water until dissolved. Allow to cool. Mix cheese, yogurt, icing sugar and mashed fruit in a bowl and fold in the gelatine mixture. Pour mixture over biscuits, cover and refrigerate for a couple of hours. Serve with some whipped cream or a splash of chosen fruit.

Could serve 6 but more satisfyingly 4.

# Tomato Soup with a Twist

*This is a good recipe when you find tomatoes cheap to buy.*

**2 lbs. tomatoes (the soft variety not hard salad type)**
**1 tablespoon sunflower oil    1 medium onion, finely chopped**
**2 cloves of garlic crushed (optional)**
**1 tablespoon tomato paste    ½ teaspoon sugar**
**2 pints of water**
**1 tablespoon balsamic vinegar**
**Salt and pepper to taste**

Skin tomatoes by dunking them in boiling water for 1–2 minutes, then dunk them in cold water to loosen the skin. Peel skins off and chop roughly. In a large deep pan heat the oil and fry onion and garlic until tender. Add water tomato and paste and simmer for 10–15 minutes. Add salt and pepper and sugar and simmer for another 5 minutes. With a hand blender process the soup, then add the balsamic vinegar. Serve with local fresh bread. Serves 4.

# METRIC CONVERSIONS

The weights, measures and oven temperatures used in the preceding recipes can be easily converted to their metric equivalents. The conversions listed below are only approximate, having been rounded up or down as may be appropriate.

## Weights

| Avoirdupois | Metric |
|---|---|
| 1 oz. | just under 30 grams |
| 4 oz. (¼ lb.) | app. 115 grams |
| 8 oz. (½ lb.) | app. 230 grams |
| 1 lb. | 454 grams |

## Liquid Measures

| Imperial | Metric |
|---|---|
| 1 tablespoon (liquid only) | 20 millilitres |
| 1 fl. oz. | app. 30 millilitres |
| 1 gill (¼ pt.) | app. 145 millilitres |
| ½ pt. | app. 285 millilitres |
| 1 pt. | app. 570 millilitres |
| 1 qt. | app. 1.140 litres |

## Oven Temperatures

| | °Fahrenheit | Gas Mark | °Celsius |
|---|---|---|---|
| Slow | 300 | 2 | 150 |
| | 325 | 3 | 170 |
| Moderate | 350 | 4 | 180 |
| | 375 | 5 | 190 |
| | 400 | 6 | 200 |
| Hot | 425 | 7 | 220 |
| | 450 | 8 | 230 |
| | 475 | 9 | 240 |

**Flour as specified in these recipes refers to plain flour unless otherwise described.**